MARTHA WASHINGTON: A BRIEF BIOGRAPHY

BY

ELLEN MCCALLISTER CLARK

Published by the
Mount Vernon Ladies' Association
and distributed by
The University of Virginia Press

This publication was made possible by
a generous grant from
M. Jacqueline and John J. McDonnell, Jr.

This book is a revised and much-expanded version of the author's essay, "The Life of Martha Washington," which was published as the Introduction to *"Worthy Partner": The Papers of Martha Washington,* compiled by Joseph E. Fields (Westport, CT: Greenwood Press, 1994).

For additional information about Martha Washington please visit www.mountvernon.org

The Mount Vernon Ladies' Association
P.O. Box 110
Mount Vernon, Virginia 22121

Cover illustrations:
Martha Dandridge Custis, copy by Adrian Lamb, 1981,
after the original by John Wollaston, circa 1756,
owned by Washington and Lee University.
Martha Washington by Charles Willson Peale, 1776

Back Cover:
Washington and His Family by Thomas Prichard Rossiter

Opposite:
Martha Washington by James Peale, 1796

ISBN: 0-931917-39-5

*"She reminded me of the Roman matrons
of whom I had read so much, and I thought that
she well deserved to be the companion and friend
of the greatest man of the age."*

PIERRE ETIENNE DU PONCEAU,
recalling a visit with Martha Washington
at Mount Vernon in November 1780.

A depiction of the marriage of Martha Dandridge Custis and George Washington by Claude Regnier after Junius Brutus Stearns, 1854.

*I*n many ways, Martha Dandridge Custis Washington represented the ideal woman of the new American republic. She was not born of the aristocracy, but she gained the admiration and respect of all classes of people. She was devoted to her family and home, but she readily made personal sacrifices to join her husband in his public duties. During the Revolution, which she referred to as "our cause," she gave up the comforts of Mount Vernon to travel every year to General Washington's winter quarters. During his presidential administration, she was called both dignified and democratic as she forged the role of the president's wife that would be followed for generations to come. She neither sought nor relished her public positions, but carried out the duties that were thrust upon her with enormous consideration and care. Her simple appearance bespoke quality rather than ostentation, and after the Revolution she set a patriotic example by wearing American-made clothes.

As her life progressed from colonial matron to national icon, the constancy of her personality gave her strength and balance. "I have learnt from experience," she told a friend in 1789, "that the greater part of our happiness or misery depends upon our dispositions, and not upon our circumstances."[1] Abigail Adams, who was never too free with compliments, wrote to her sister that "Mrs. Washington is one of those unassuming characters which create Love and Esteem," and admitted that when in her presence she found herself "much more deeply impressed than I ever did before their Majesties of Britain."[2] Years later, a former Mount

Vernon slave told Mrs. Washington's great granddaughter that "she could not see why so much fuss was made over 'the Genl, he was only a man!'," but Mrs. Washington's beauty and goodness had been unmatched.[3]

This rare engraving of Martha Washington was created by J. Norman and published by John Coles of Boston in 1782. Photo by Marlor.

A family Bible records the birth of Martha Dandridge on June 2, 1731, "between 12 and one o'clock."[4] The oldest child of John and Frances Jones Dandridge of New Kent County, Virginia, she started life as part of a respectable, but by no means wealthy, family whose status has been described as part of the "second tier" of planters within the stratified Virginia society of the time. Her father John Dandridge (1700-1756), the son of a master artisan from London, immigrated to Virginia with an older brother William in 1714. The Dandridge brothers first settled in Hampton, Virginia, and began a rapid rise as merchants and landowners. In 1730, John purchased 500 acres on the south bank of the Pamunkey River in New Kent County and built a house, which he named Chestnut Grove. On July 22 of that year he married Frances Jones (1710-1785), a second-generation Virginian whose grandfather, Reverend Rowland Jones (1640-1688), had served as the first pastor of Bruton Parish Church in Williamsburg.

Following Martha's birth in 1731, the Dandridge household at Chestnut Grove expanded to eight children with the addition of three boys and four girls: John (1732-1749), William (1734-1776), Bartholomew (1737-1785), Anna Maria (1739-1777), Frances (1744-1758), Elizabeth (1749-18—), and Mary (1756-1763). As the eldest, Martha undoubtedly had a role raising her younger brothers and sisters. Her letters as an adult to her surviving siblings reveal close and affectionate family ties, and she was a doting aunt to her many nieces and nephews.

Little is known about Martha's childhood, but it is fair to assume that her education was typical for a girl of her social class in colonial Virginia. Her father had sufficient education to conduct the business of Clerk of New Kent County, a position he held for twenty-five years. Her mother's father, Orlando Jones, was a graduate of the College of William and Mary and member of the Virginia House of Burgesses who assembled a notable private library. Lessons in reading, writing and arithmetic were probably conducted at home, possibly by itinerant tutors who traveled from plantation to plantation. From the women in her family Martha and her sisters would have received solid training in domestic arts and household management. Religion would also have had an essential place in family life. The Dandridges were undoubtedly regulars in attendance at their parish church, St. Peter's, where John Dandridge served on the vestry. While it is not known what specific books Martha might have read growing up, a list of titles known to have been ordered for or owned by her in adulthood reveals a range of interests from theology and philosophy to travel and the popular novels of the day.

Music and dancing were also considered crucial elements of a young person's training – Philip Fithian, a tutor on the plantation of Robert Carter in the 1770s, observed that in Virginia such "ornamental" skills were "a necessary qualification for a person to appear even decent in Company." There is evidence that Martha was an accomplished equestrienne in her youth, and she appreciated good horses and continued riding for exercise as an adult.

Whatever the extent of her formal education, Martha Dandridge by all accounts grew up to be a sensible and

Martha Dandridge Custis, copy by Adrian Lamb, 1981, after the original by John Wollaston, circa 1756, owned by Washington and Lee University. Photograph by Ted Vaughan.

cultivated young woman, well prepared to take on the expected responsibilities of a wife and plantation mistress. Still, it must have seemed her very good fortune when at the age of eighteen she attracted the attention of Daniel Parke Custis (1711-1757), a vestryman at her church and a member of one of Virginia's most prominent families. It was not an easy courtship. A thirty-eight-year-old bachelor, Daniel was the son of a wealthy and eccentric widower, John Custis, who so tightly controlled the family fortune that he is known to have denied his son funds for the basic management of his farm operations while giving away slaves, silver and furnishings to neighbors. It was rumored that, in a fit of rage, he had drafted a new will that left his entire estate to a favored slave boy named Jack, who is believed to have been his illegitimate son.[5] When the elder Custis first learned of Daniel's interest in Martha, he is reported to have strenuously objected on the grounds that "Mr. Dandridge's daughter was inferior to his Son... in point of Fortune."[6] Although several influential family friends sought to intervene, it was finally Martha herself who charmed the old gentleman with a "prudent speech," so that he not only reversed his position, he declared to attorney John Power that he was so "enamored of her character" that he would rather have Daniel marry Martha Dandridge "than any lady in Virginia."[7] Already in failing health, John Custis wrote a new will assuring that Daniel would receive the majority of his estate and, before he could change his mind again, he died on November 22, 1749.

*M*artha Dandridge and Daniel Parke Custis were married by the Reverend Chichely Corbin Thacker on May 15, 1750, probably at the bride's home, as was the custom of the time. The couple settled on the Custis estate, White House, on the Pamunkey River, about thirty miles from Williamsburg. It was there that their four children were born in quick succession. The first two, Daniel Parke Custis (b. 1751) and Frances Parke Custis (b. 1753), died in early childhood. A second son and daughter, John Parke Custis (b. 1754) and Martha Parke Custis (b. 1756), became the focus of their doting parents, who spared no expense for their comfort and well-being.

Although he was freed from his difficult father's control, Daniel Parke Custis saw his large inheritance encumbered by lawsuits, loans and other complications. The greatest obstacle was a twenty-year-old claim by the estate of Thomas Dunbar against John Custis that remained unsettled. Dunbar was married to Lucy Chester, an illegitimate daughter of Colonel Daniel Parke (1669-1709) who was also the father of Daniel's mother, Frances Parke Custis. Colonel Parke had served as an aide to the Duke of Marlborough and had delivered the news of the victory at Blenheim to Queen Anne, who rewarded him with a prize of 1,000 guineas, a portrait of herself set in diamonds and the governorship of the Leeward Islands. Taking office in Antigua in 1705, Parke ran an administration so tainted with scandal and political corruption that within five years he was killed in a violent insurrection. His will, drawn up in January 1709, left his extensive Leeward

Island property to one-year-old Lucy Chester, while directing that his "daughter Frances Parke pay out of my estate in Virginia and Hampshire [England] all my legal debts and bequests." When Lucy Chester at age eleven married Thomas Dunbar of Antigua, they took on the surname Parke to cement their claim on her father's estate. Legal jousting over the distribution of property and responsibilities for Colonel Parke's vast debts outlasted the lives of all the principals and became even more complicated and contentious in the succeeding generations. In 1754, Daniel Parke Custis wrote to his friend and attorney John Mercer that he "had not the quantity of money as you & some others imagined" as long as the Dunbar suit loomed over him.[8]

But like his father, he would not live to see it settled. On July 8, 1757, after seven years of marriage, Daniel Parke Custis died suddenly, probably from a heart attack. Leaving no will, his large estate, appraised at more than £23,000, was divided among his twenty-six-year-old widow and her two young children. As executrix, Martha Custis found herself responsible for the management of more than 17,500 acres of land and 300 slaves located in the counties of New Kent, Northampton, York, King William and Hanover, and in James City and Williamsburg. With the help of her husband's manager, James Valentine, and several trusted advisors she carried on the Custis family's thriving tobacco business and grappled with the estate's unsettled legal and financial entanglements.

The earliest known letters of Martha Custis date from this period, written to the London merchants with whom her husband did business. "I take the Opportunity to inform you of the great misfortune I have met with in the loss of my late Husband," she wrote to John Hanbury and Company on August 20, 1757. "As I now have the Administration of his Estate and the management of his Affairs of all sorts [,] I shall be glad to continue the correspondence which Mr. Custis carried on with you...." On the same day she also wrote to Robert Cary and Company: "I shall yearly ship a considerable part of the Tobacco I make to you which I shall take care to have as good as possible and hope you will do your endeavour to get me a good price." To both firms she noted that she would continue her late husband's accounts "in the same manner as if he were living."[9]

Martha Dandridge Custis would not have to manage her affairs alone for long. Evidence that the wealthy young widow sparked the interest of more than one bachelor is found in a letter of John Tayloe to William Byrd III written on April 4, 1758: "C.C. is very gay & says he has attacked the widow Custis." At least one historian has identified the suitor as Charles Carter (1707-1764) of "Cleve" near Port Royal, Virginia, a member of the House of Burgesses and, at age fifty-one, a recent widower.[10] Although it is not known how Mrs. Custis responded to this "attack," at the time the letter was written she had already begun a courtship with a tall young colonel named George Washington. Like her, he came from a moderately affluent Tidewater Virginia family. As the eldest son of his father's second marriage, he had had limited opportunities for formal education and inheritance, and he had been on his own since adolescence to carve his place in the world. But now, at age twenty-six, Colonel Washington was the highest-ranking officer of the Virginia provincial troops and had already achieved fame and international recognition for his heroic exploits during Great Britain's ongoing war against the French in the New World.

There is no contemporary account of their first meeting, though it is likely that they would at least have known of each other in the close society of Williamsburg and its nearby plantations. Martha's grandson, George Washington Parke Custis, in his memoirs, left a wonderfully romantic account of their immediate mutual attraction when the two were introduced at Poplar Grove, the home of Richard Chamberlayne, in New Kent County in early 1758. Whatever the actual circumstances, Washington's visit to the Chamberlayne plantation in mid-March of that year is confirmed in his ledger book as one of the stops he made during a trip to Williamsburg where, on leave from his military command, he sought medical advice for a long and debilitating bout with dysentery. One week later, on March 25, 1758, his accounts record gratuities given to Mrs. Custis's servants when he called on her at her home. The exact date of their engagement is not known, but there may be a clue in Washington's April order to his London factor, "By the first Ship bound to any part of Virginia... As much of the best superfine Blue Cotton Velvet as will make a Coat, Waistcoat & Breeches for a Tall Man....six p[ai]r of the neatest Shoes...[and] Six pairs of gloves."[11] It was probably at about the same time that Mrs. Custis also sent out an order to have her favorite "night gown" dyed a fashionable color, and to have

14

a seamstress make "one Genteel suite of cloths for my self to be grave but not Extravagent nor to be mourning."[12]

His health much restored, Washington returned to his military duties as commander at Fort Loudoun in Winchester, where preparations were being made to move against the French forces occupying Fort Duquesne, a strategic stronghold located at the juncture of the Monongahela, Allegheny and Ohio rivers in western Pennsylvania. On the orders of British Quartermaster General Sir John St. Clair, Washington returned to Williamsburg in late May to confer with the president of the House of Burgesses on support for the forthcoming campaign. On June 5, he visited Martha Custis again before heading north to Winchester. In addition to a tip of fourteen shillings, six pence to the Custis servants, Washington's ledger records payment of sixteen shillings for a "Ring from Phila[delphia]."

As with every wartime engagement, the couple faced immediate uncertainties about their future. There is no documentary evidence to support the tradition that Washington promised to resign his commission as part of his pledge to Martha Custis, but clearly he was anticipating a time when he would return to civilian life. In July 1758, he stood for election to represent the citizens of Frederick County in the House of Burgesses. Although his obligations to his regiment kept him from being present at the polls on election day, with the help of his friends and an ample supply of spirits supplied to the voters, he won his seat by a comfortable margin.

But there was little time for celebration. Washington's immediate concern was the escalating campaign to reclaim the Ohio Forks for the British Crown. He was now serving under the command of Brigadier General John Forbes, who had been sent from England to command the provincial forces of the middle colonies. Although there were bitter tensions between them over the best route to take the army west, Forbes recognized Washington's expertise in wilderness warfare and placed him in command of the advance brigade with the temporary rank of brigadier general. Washington's assignment was to lead the way through the wilderness cutting the route for the main army to follow. It was a slow and arduous trek that became more desperate and dangerous as winter closed in. Finally on November 24, with the army within fifteen miles of its target, word came from Indian scouts that the French had abandoned Fort Duquesne rather than risk a siege. In a surprising but welcome anti-climax, the provincial forces took over the burned-out fort without firing a shot, and Washington headed south again.

Martha Washington's wedding shoes were purple satin with silver trimmings. Photo by Taylor Lewis.

It was Christmastime when Washington finally reached Williamsburg, where he made the case for much-needed provisions for the Virginia soldiers garrisoned at the captured fort. With this last act on behalf of his men, he tendered his resignation as commander of the Virginia Regiments. Upon hearing the news, twenty-seven of his fellow officers signed their names to a "humble address" in which they lamented the loss of "such an Excellent Commander, such a sincere Friend, and so affable a Companion... the actuating Soul of the whole Corps."[13] In later life, Washington recalled that their affectionate farewell had "affected him exceedingly."

George Washington married Martha Dandridge Custis on Twelfth Night, January 6, 1759, at the bride's home, White House. The Reverend David Mossom, rector of St. Peter's Church, officiated. At five feet tall the petite bride was more than a foot shorter than her dashing groom, who was described by a friend as "being straight as an Indian, measuring six feet two in his stockings, and weighing 175 pounds...." According to her descendants, the bride wore a "petticoat of white silk interwoven with silver. The overdress, open in front, a deep yellow brocade with rich lace in the neck and sleeves. Ornaments of pearls. Her shoes were purple satin with silver trimmings." The retired colonel is believed to have appeared in civilian dress – possibly in a wedding suit made of the blue velvet ordered from London the previous spring. Many decades later an elderly family slave recalled the event to Martha's grandson: "Many of the grandest gentlemen, in their gold lace, were at the wedding, but none looked like the man himself!"[14] When news of the event reached Washington's former regiment at Fort Loudoun, his friend Robert Stewart wrote: "I … beg leave to present my hearty Congratulations on your happy union with the Lady that all agree has long been the just object of your affections—may you long enjoy all the felicity you propos'd by it, or that Matrimony can possibly afford—Be so good as to offer my Complements in the most respectful and obliging Terms to Your Lady (a new Stile indeed) and tho' she has rob'd me and many others of the greatest satisfaction we ever had or can enjoy in this Service yet none can be more sollicitous for her happiness."[15]

The newlyweds remained in New Kent County for the first months of their married life. They traveled frequently to Williamsburg, where the new Mrs. Washington, already a well-known figure in society, now made her debut as the wife of the most talked-about man in the colonies. On February 22, his twenty-seventh birthday, George Washington took his seat in the Virginia House of Burgesses. Four days later, his peers in the House passed a resolution thanking their new member "late Colonel of the First Virginia Regiment, for his faithful Services to his Majesty, and this Colony, and for his brave and steady behavior, from the first Encroachments and hostilities of the French and their Indians, to his Resignation, after the happy Reduction of Fort DuQuesne."

Washington was assigned to the Committee of Propositions and Grievances, which oversaw matters of business and politics, under the chairmanship of Charles Carter of "Cleve." The House also looked to the war veteran for advice on legislation to increase the strength of the First

Virginia Regiment and provide "aid to his Majesty for the better Protection and Defence of this Colony." After weeks of debate, a compromise bill was finally put to a vote and was passed on April 2. Having done his part for his former comrades-in-arms and eager to get on with his spring planting, Washington applied for and was granted a leave of absence two weeks before the session was to adjourn.

Within days, Washington had packed up his household in New Kent County and set out with his bride and young family for Mount Vernon, his estate on the upper reaches of the Potomac River. They were already on the road when he sent an urgent message to his overseer that the long-vacant house was to be "prepared in the best manner you can for our coming." Washington had become proprietor of this family property in 1754, when at the age of twenty-two he first leased about 2,500 acres, including a simple story-and-a half cottage, from the widow of his elder half-brother, Lawrence Washington. Even before he gained full ownership of the estate in 1761, Washington began the expansion and improvement of the house and property that would continue for the rest of his life. By the time Mrs. Washington first saw her new home, the original house had already been raised to two-and-a-half stories, although it still lacked the north and south wings of the mansion house that exists today. The first floor had been embellished with fine paneling and other architectural details, and the exterior siding had been rusticated to give the appearance of stone. Although at this point Mount Vernon was still a far cry from the elegance the former Mrs. Custis had known back in New Kent County, she seems to have moved happily into the nucleus of what would evolve over the next forty years to become one of the best known homes in America.

The first fifteen years of the Washingtons' marriage have been called the "golden years" at Mount Vernon. A few months after they took residence, Washington wrote to his English agent, "I am now I believe fixed at this Seat with an agreeable Consort for life and hope to find more happiness in retirement than I ever experienced amidst a wide and bustling World."[16] While he surely had no idea how impermanent this "retirement" would be, he devoted himself to his family and farm. As would be expected of a husband of a widow, he took over the management of all of the Custis estate matters, maintaining careful separate accounts for both of his stepchildren, John Parke Custis, called Jacky by the family, and Martha Parke Custis, called Patsy, which was also Washington's nickname for his bride. Although George and Martha Washington would not have children of their own, he became a devoted guardian to Mrs. Washington's children, who called him "Pappa."

The Custis children's inheritance enabled Washington to provide amply for their comfort and education. His early accounts of expenditures on their behalf are filled with orders for clothing, toys, and books. In 1761, he ordered a spinet for Patsy from one of the best harpsichord makers in London (imploring his factor "not to let it be known it is intended for Exportation"). A few years later he purchased a violin and German flute for Jacky. By then both Custis children were

Mrs. Washington possessed an extensive wardrobe, including this brown dress. Photo by Edward Owen.

studying music with John Stadler, a traveling music teacher who visited Mount Vernon about once a month. Washington's accounts for 1766 show that for a time Mrs. Washington joined in the lessons, though by the following year payments to Mr. Stadler were for Master and Miss Custis only. A tutor, Walter Macgowan, was hired in 1761 to oversee a "classical" education for the children. Shortly after the tutor's arrival, Washington sent out an order for "2 Copies of the Rudimt. of the Latin F. 2 Phaedrus Fables, 2 Salust, Horace, the Gram'l Exercises, Erasmus, Latin & Eng'h Dic'y" on the account of Jacky and Patsy Custis, who were then only eight and six years old.

Although her husband now took the lead in their business dealings, Mrs. Washington maintained a close and involved interest in financial matters. Her taste for elegant things was tempered by a Virginia housewife's frugality. In an order sent to a milliner, Mrs. Shelbury, in London in 1764, Mrs. Washington wrote that she would have no objections to receiving clothes for Patsy that were "more genteel and proper" than the ones sent a year earlier, "provided it is done with frugality, for as she is only nine years old a superfluity, or expence in dress would be altogether unnecessary." Well aware that colonial customers were often overcharged for inferior goods from England, she scrutinized shipments when they arrived and did not hesitate to complain if their contents did not meet her standards. In 1772, she wrote to Mrs. S. Thorpe, another London milliner, about "some very hard bargains" she had received through her London factor, Cary & Sons. While she had ordered a "hands[om]e Suit of Brussels Lace to cost £20" for her daughter, she had received only part of her order and the items that arrived were of a quality "as can be bought in ye milliners Shops here." She would try again with another order, she wrote, but "if you cant afford to see a much better barg[ai]n in these ... I should hope [that] Mr. Cary will try elsewhere."[17]

During these early years at Mount Vernon, Mrs. Washington became expert at her role as mistress of a busy and ever-expanding plantation. Her domain was the mansion house, kitchen, smokehouse, spinning house and washhouse, all of which she managed with care and efficiency. One of her specialties was the hanging and curing of meat in the smokehouse. When sending a barrel of Mount Vernon hams to the Marquis de Lafayette in France, Washington wrote, "You know the Virginia Ladies value themselves on the goodness of their bacon."[18] Lund Washington, a kinsman who managed Mount Vernon during the years of the Revolution, noted that "Mrs. Washington's Charitable disposition increases in the same proportion with her meat House."[19]

Mrs. Washington's portion of her first husband's estate included the ownership of nearly 100 slaves. Although it is not known exactly how many of these "dower" slaves came with her initially, over the years a number of them were brought to live and work at Mount Vernon. In 1759, her household staff numbered eleven: two cooks, two waiters, two laundresses, one seamstress and a personal servant for Mrs. Washington, her husband and both of her children.[20] Her attitudes about slavery seem to be very much in keeping with what would be expected of a woman of her time and station in life – there is no evidence in these early years that she questioned the existence of the institution that she had known since birth, but at the same time she displayed genuine concern and even affection for certain individuals who were bound to her in servitude.

Her immediate family took her greatest attention, however, and she can only be described as a doting mother. She worried over her children's many illnesses and was miserable at any separation. In 1762, she wrote to her sister of a trip she took to visit Washington family relatives in Westmoreland County: "I carred my little patt with me and left Jackey at home for a trial to see how well I coud stay without him[.] though we are gon but wone fortnight I was quite impatiant to get home[.] if I at any time heard the doggs barke or a noise out I thought thair was a person sent for me[.] I often fansied he was sick or some accident had happened to him so that I think it is impossable for me to leave him...."[21]

Patsy Custis was, like her mother, amiable and pretty, and was well accomplished in music and needlework, but from an early age she suffered from what were probably epileptic seizures that came with greater frequency as she grew into adolescence. She was treated by many doctors, was made to wear an iron ring believed to have curative powers, and was taken to Berkeley Springs in what is now West Virginia in search of a cure, but her ailment was beyond the help of eighteenth-century medicine. In June of 1773, when she was seventeen, she was seized with one of her fits and died at Mount Vernon, a blow that in Washington's words "reduced my poor wife to the lowest ebb of Misery."[22]

Mrs. Washington's sadness was deepened by the fact that her only other living child was away at college at the time of Patsy's death. Jacky Custis was handsome and engaging but, much to the dismay of his stepfather, the boy who had been given every advantage lacked ambition and direction as he grew into manhood. Washington privately blamed Jacky's laziness on his overly indulgent mother, and he seems to have been unable or unwilling to enforce a stronger discipline himself. Even when she was consumed with worry over Patsy's deteriorating health, Mrs. Washington's anxiety for her son's welfare bordered on the irrational. Not only could she not bear any separation, when Jacky was to be inoculated against smallpox, it was arranged for his mother to be spared all knowledge of it until the deed was performed and he had fully recovered.

In 1768, when Jacky was fourteen, Mrs. Washington was persuaded to let him go away school to study under the tutelage of the Reverend Jonathan Boucher in Caroline County (and later in Annapolis, Maryland). In making arrangements for his enrollment, Washington revealed his hopes for his stepson, "a boy of good genius… untainted in his Morals, & of innocent Manners…. he will be put entirely, and absolutely under your Tuition, and direction to manage as you think proper in all respects…. he is a promising boy; the last of his Family — & will possess a very large Fortune — add to this my anxiety to make him fit for more useful purposes, than a horse Racer &ca."[23] Over the next several years, Washington and Boucher corresponded about Jacky's rather shaky progress, which was frequently interrupted by extended trips home. Although Washington was candid about his concerns for Jacky's future, Boucher surely crossed the line of parent-teacher decorum when he wrote to him in December 1770, "I must confess to You I never did in my Life know a youth so exceedingly indolent or so surprisingly voluptuous: one wd suppose nature had intended Him for some Asiatic Prince." Two years later, the Reverend admitted defeat: "It is certainly expedient to remove Mr. Custis to some place of publick Education and speedily."[24]

After considering several colleges, including William and Mary, Pennsylvania and Princeton, Jack, as he was now known, was enrolled at King's College in New York City, which had been Boucher's recommendation. His mother had expressed a preference for his attending a school closer to home, but she seems to have been in agreement with the necessity of his continuing his education. She had been especially hurt to learn that before he left Boucher's school, Jack had become secretly engaged to a sixteen-year-old girl from Maryland, Eleanor Calvert. Although the Washingtons were quickly won over by "Miss Nelly's amiable qualifications," Washington wrote to the girl's father, "[Jack's] youth, inexperience, and unripened Education, is, & will be insuperable obstacles in my eye, to the completion of the Marriage."[25]

With a postponement of the wedding agreed upon, Washington escorted Jack to New York to begin his studies in May of 1773. He was there only a little over a month when he received the tragic news of his "dear only sister's death." He came home for vacation in September with glowing reports from his professors, but with his own determination to follow his heart and marry Nelly Calvert. A glimpse of family dynamics is revealed in Washington's grim letter to the president of King's College informing him that his stepson would not be returning to school: "The favourable account you was pleas'd to transmit me of Mr Custis's conduct at College, gave me very great satisfaction...but these hopes are at an end; & at length, I have yielded, contrary to my judgment, & much against my wishes, to his quitting College; in order that he may enter soon into a new scene of Life, which I think he would be much fitter for some years hence, than now; but having his own inclination-the desires of his mother-& the acquiescence of almost all his relatives, to encounter, I did not care, as he is the last of the family, to push my opposition too far; & therefore have submitted to a Kind of necessity."[26]

In February of 1774, Jack married Nelly Calvert at her home Mount Airy across the Potomac River in Maryland. His stepfather George Washington attended the ceremony and stayed over an extra day to share in the festivities, but his mother, still in mourning for his sister, remained at home.

George Washington had been successively reelected to the House of Burgesses and was now representing his home county of Fairfax. He had been an outspoken critic of the Stamp Act of 1765 and continued to closely follow the sharpening debate over colonial rights. In May of 1774, when news of the closing of the port at Boston and other "intolerable acts" reached Williamsburg, the Burgesses voted a day of fasting and prayer to protest. When the Royal Governor promptly dissolved the Assembly, the delegates, Washington among them, resumed their meeting at a tavern to continue the debate. Back at home in July, Washington chaired a meeting of local patriots that drafted an influential list of demands known as the "Fairfax Resolves." The following month, Washington was appointed to be one of Virginia's representatives at the first Continental Congress, and on August 31, he set off from Mount Vernon for Philadelphia in the company of fellow delegates Patrick Henry and Edmund Pendleton. The only surviving record of

Mrs. Washington's reaction to the gathering political storm is found in a letter Pendleton wrote describing his stopover at Mount Vernon: "I was most pleased with Mrs. Washington and her spirit. She seemed ready to make any sacrifice and was cheerful though I knew she felt anxious. She talked like a Spartan mother to her son going to battle. 'I hope you will stand firm – I know George will,' she said. The dear little woman was busy from morning to night in domestic duties, but she gave us much time in conversation and affording us entertainment. When we set off in the morning, she stood in the door and cheered us with the good words, 'God be with you gentlemen.'"[27]

*I*n May of 1775, Mrs. Washington bade farewell to her husband again as he rode away from Mount Vernon to attend the second Continental Congress in Philadelphia. The next month Congress appointed him Commander-in-Chief of the newly formed Continental Army raised for the defense of the American colonies. Only three letters written by George Washington to his wife survive[28], but it seems more than coincidental that two of them, written on this momentous occasion that changed their lives forever, were found tucked behind a desk drawer after her death. On June 18, 1775, he wrote to break the news of his appointment in words he could express only to his wife:

> *I now set down to write you on a subject which fills me*
> *with inexpressible concern – and this concern is greatly*
> *aggravated and Increased, when I reflect upon the*

*uneasiness I know it will give you – It has been
determined in Congress that the whole Army raised for the
defence of the American Cause shall be put under my
care, and that it is necessary for me to proceed
immediately to Boston to take upon me the command of
it. You may believe me my dear Patcy when I assure you,
in the most solemn manner, that, so far from seeking this
appointment I have used every endeavour in my power to
avoid it, not only from my unwillingness to part with you
and the Family, but from a consciousness of its being a
trust too great for my Capacity and that I should enjoy
more real happiness and felicity in one month with you, at
home, than I have the most distant prospect of reaping
abroad, if my stay were to be Seven times Seven
years ....[20]*

While expressing hopes that he would return home in the fall,
Washington went on to tell her that "as Life is always
uncertain, and common prudence dictates to every Man the
necessity of settling his temporal Concerns whilst it is in his
power," he had arranged to have a will drafted in Philadelphia,
which he now enclosed with the letter. Over the next few days
Washington wrote to several family members about his concern
for Mrs. Washington. "I shall hope that my Friends will visit,
& endeavour to keep up the Spirits of my Wife as much as
they can," he told his brother, "as my departure will, I know be
a cutting stroke upon her."[30]

On his last morning in Philadelphia, he took up his
pen to write to his wife again:

This print of Mrs. Washington in her later years was inspired by an original painting by Chappel.

Phila. June 23d 1775

My dearest,

*As I am within a few minutes of leaving this City, I could
not think of departing from it without dropping you a line,
especially as I do know whether it may be in my power to
write you again till I get to the Camp at Boston – I go
fully trusting in that Providence, which has been more
bountiful to me than I deserve, & in full confidence of a
happy Meeting with you sometime in the Fall – I have no
time to add more, as I am surrounded with Company to
take leave of me – I retain an unalterable affection for you,
which neither time nor distance can change. My best love
to Jack and Nelly and regard for the rest of the family
concludes me with the utmost truth & sincerity,*

Yr entire

G°:Washington[31]

Martha Washington's devotion and behind-the-scenes
support of her husband in all of his pursuits characterized her
entire married life; however, it is during the period of the
American Revolution that she also emerges as a selfless,
courageous and patriotic American. Beginning in November
1775, she traveled every year to winter quarters to be with her
husband and to give what assistance she could to the soldiers
in camp. Her first trip north, from Mount Vernon to
Cambridge, Massachusetts, took nearly a month and included
a weeklong stop in Philadelphia, where she was surprised by the
warm reception that awaited the wife of the Commander-in-
Chief. To a friend back in Alexandria she wrote: "I don't doubt
but you have see[n] the Figuer our arrival made in the

Philadelphia paper – and I left it in as great pomp as if I had been a very great somebody."

Having arrived safely at Cambridge on December 11, she went on in the same letter to report her first impressions of life on the front lines: "I have waited some days to collect something to tell, but allas there is nothing but what you will find in the papers – every person seems to be cheerfull and happy hear, — some days we have a number of cannon and shells from Boston and Bunkers Hill, but it does not seem to surprise any one but me; I confess I shudder every time I hear the sound of a gun …I just took a look at pore Boston & Charlestown from prospect Hill[.] Charlestown has only a few chimneys standing in it, thare seems to be a number of very fine buildings in Boston but god knows how long they will stand; they are pulling up all the warfs for firewood – to me that has never see[n] any thing of war the preparations are very terable indeed, but I endever to keep my fears to myself as well as I can."[32]

Mrs. Washington had been accompanied on her journey to Cambridge by her son Jack, his wife Nelly, George Lewis, a nephew of her husband's, and Mrs. Horatio Gates, the wife the army's adjutant general. The entourage quickly made themselves an integral part of Washington's "military family." Mrs. Washington received and called upon the other officers' wives who had come to camp, as well as many prominent New Englanders who were eager to meet the lady from Virginia. She made a particularly good impression on Mercy Otis Warren, who described their meeting in a letter to Abigail Adams: "I took a Ride to Cambridge and waited on Mrs. Washington… I was Receiv'd with that politness and Respect shewn in a first interview among the well bred and with the Ease and Cordiallity of Friendship of a much Earlier date. If you wish to hear more of this Ladys Character I will tell you I think the Complacency of her Manners speaks at once the Benevolence of her Heart, and her affability, Candor and Gentleness Quallify her to soften the hours of private Life or to sweeten the Care of the Hero and smooth the Rugged scenes of War...."[33]

Over the winter at Cambridge, Washington had held the British who occupied Boston at bay while he reorganized the troops under his command. The arrival of cannon and mortar captured from Fort Ticonderoga so greatly strengthened the American position that the British decided to move their offensive elsewhere. In January 1776, Mrs. Washington reported to her sister "A few days a goe [British General Sir Henry] Clinton, with several companyes Sailed out of Boston Harbor to what place distant for, we cannot find out.... If [he] is gon to New York, [American General Charles] Lee is there before him and I hope he will give him a very warm reception."[34] Clinton in fact was heading for the Carolinas, but it would not be long before British Commander-in-Chief General William Howe would order his all of his troops out of Boston and set his sights on New York City.

Following the British evacuation in March, the Washingtons traveled south to New York, and then to Philadelphia where the General reported in to Congress. Mrs. Washington had put off her own inoculation for smallpox for years, but her husband finally persuaded her to have it done now that her travels put her at greater risk. On May 31, Washington wrote to his brother that "Mrs. Washington is now under Innoculation... this is the 13th day, and she has very few Pustules," adding that she was not yet writing letters herself out of concern over "conveying the Infection."[35] Jack Custis, who had left for Maryland with his pregnant wife some weeks earlier, now wrote, in a reversal of family roles, of his relief at hearing of the speedy recovery of "so dear a Mother."

General Washington had returned to New York City on June 6 to prepare for the inevitable British attack. Mrs. Washington joined him there briefly after her recovery, but with the landing of the British forces on Staten Island she returned again to the relative safety of Philadelphia. She was still there in August when she received the news from Jack and Nelly of the birth of her first surviving grandchild, Elizabeth Parke Custis, "as fine a Healthy, fat Baby as ever was born."[36]

Back home at Mount Vernon in late September, Mrs. Washington again turned her attention to her expanding family and domestic concerns. When he left for the war, Washington had turned the general management of his estate over to his cousin Lund Washington, who was now eager to show the mistress of the house a number of improvements that had gone forward in her absence. Jack, Nelly and baby Eliza, now in residence, undoubtedly provided comfort and diversion as Mrs. Washington anxiously followed the news of her husband's retreat across New Jersey and dramatic turnaround at Trenton and Princeton.

In March 1777, Mrs. Washington traveled north again to join her husband at winter quarters in Morristown, New Jersey. Their reunion made a strong impression on a number of observers, among them General Nathanael Greene, who reported to his wife, "Mrs. Washington and Mrs. Bland from

Virginia are at Camp, happy with their better halves. Mrs. Washington is excessive fond of the General and he of her. ...."[37] Martha Dangerfield Bland also made note their happiness as she described the social life at camp to her sister-in-law: "... Now let me speak of our Nobel and Agreable Commander (for he commands both Sexes), one by his Excellent Skill in Military Matters, the other by his ability politeness and attention....He is generally busy in the forenoon – but from dinner till night he is free for all company. His Worthy Lady seems to be in perfect felicity while she is by the side of her Old Man as she calls him. We often make partys on Horse back the Genl, his lady, Miss Livingstone & his Aid de Camps...at which time General Washington throws of[f] the hero—and takes on the chatty agreable companion – he can be downright impudent sometimes – such impudence, Fanny, as you and I like...."[38]

Winter after winter, as conditions grew increasingly rough, Mrs. Washington became indispensable as a nurse and comfort to Washington and his men. "Greatly was she beloved in the army," her grandson wrote years later. "Her many intercessions with the chief for the pardon of offenders, and her kindness to the sick and wounded, caused her annual arrival in camp to be hailed as an event that would dissipate the gloom of the winter-quarters."[39] As the hard winter set in at Valley Forge in January 1778, Lafayette wrote to his wife that "several general officers have brought their wives to camp, and I am very envious, not of their wives (who are rather dull), but of the pleasure they have in being able to see them. General Washington has also just decided to send for his wife, a modest and respectable person, who loves her husband madly...."[40] James Thacher, an army surgeon who saw her at Middlebrook the following year, noted in his diary, "Mrs. Washington combines in an uncommon degree great dignity of manner, with the most pleasing affability, but possesses no striking marks of beauty. I learn from the Virginia officers that [she] has ever been honored as a lady of distinguished goodness ...amiable in her temper and deportment, full of benignity, benevolence and charity...."[41] But though she was surrounded by those who admired and needed her, she missed her family at Mount Vernon terribly. In a letter to Jack and Nelly, written from Middlebrook in March 1779, she wonders if everyone has forgotten her, threatening in desperation, "if you do not write, I will not write to you again."[42] Returning home as the military campaigns resumed in the spring must have renewed her, for she never let her husband down.

In the spring of 1781, the main action of the war shifted to Virginia. Mrs. Washington, then at headquarters at New Windsor, New York, and suffering from an illness, postponed her return to Mount Vernon while her husband monitored the unfolding events in their home state. She finally set out from camp in June and, after an extended stay in Philadelphia to regain her strength, arrived home in August. The following month, her husband, accompanied by his aides and French General Rochambeau, stopped at Mount Vernon for a couple of days on their march south to Yorktown. It was General Washington's first glimpse of his home in more than six years.

Jack Custis had never enlisted in the army, but he now

persuaded his stepfather to allow him to join the campaign as a volunteer aide. Jack was in good health and spirits when he wrote to his mother from Washington's headquarters on the York River on October 12, but within a few days he was stricken with camp fever. It is not clear whether he remained in Yorktown to witness the British surrender on October 19, but he was soon taken to Eltham, the home of his widowed uncle, Burwell Bassett, in New Kent County. As his condition worsened, Mrs. Washington and Nelly were summoned from Mount Vernon. General Washington rode up from Yorktown on November 5, "in time to see Mr. Custis breathe his last," he wrote to an aide. "The deep and solumn distress of the Mother, and the affliction of the Wife of this amiable young Man, requires every comfort in my power to afford them."[43]

Following burial services at Eltham, the grieving family traveled back to Mount Vernon, but for General and Mrs. Washington it would be only a brief respite. The victory at Yorktown had not ended the war, and duty called again. On November 20, the Washingtons headed north together, first to Philadelphia, where the General received the praise of Congress, and then on to new winter quarters at Newburgh, New York.

*G*eorge Washington refused a salary for his services as commander-in-chief, but applied to Congress for his expenses only. After some deliberation, he included in his final accounting a charge of £1,064.1.0 for Mrs. Washington's wartime travels between December 1775 and December 1782. One of the treasures of the Mount Vernon collection is a memorandum in Washington's hand on which he carefully tallied up his wife's traveling expenses to and from winter quarters year after year. Listing round-trip expenses from Mount Vernon to Cambridge and New York (December 1775-July 1776), Morristown (March-May 1777), Valley Forge (February-June 1778), Philadelphia and Middlebrook (December 1778-June 1779), Morristown (December 1779-June 1780), New Windsor (November 1780-June 1781) and (omitting the journey they made together from Mount Vernon) a trip home from Newburgh in July and back again in December 1782, the document provides a succinct chronology of the war as well as a testimonial to the devotion and fortitude of Martha Washington.

Mrs. Washington had barely recovered from a fever when she made her final trip home from the war, departing from Rocky Hill, near Princeton, New Jersey, in October 1783, "before the weather and roads should get bad." Eight years of hard traveling had taken their toll, she confessed in a letter to a friend a few months later, "My frequent long Journeys have not only left me without inclination to undertake another, but almost disqualified me from doing it, as I find the fatiegue is too much for me to bear."[44] Her husband remained on duty, waiting for the official news of the definitive treaty of peace, which was finally received in early November. His last military act was to lead the triumphal march into New York on the day the British evacuated the city. He soon left for Annapolis, the temporary seat of Congress, where on December 23, 1783, he resigned his commission as commander-in-chief. His obligations to his country fulfilled, he headed home to his family, reaching Mount Vernon on Christmas Eve.

"*T*he difficulties and distresses to which we have been exposed during the war must now be forgotten – we must endevor to let our ways be the way of pleasentness and all our paths Peace."[45] So wrote Martha Washington to her friend Hannah Stockton Boudinot as the new year began in 1784. The Washingtons were now engaged in putting their home and farm back in order after the long years of war. Jack Custis's death in 1781 had left his twenty-three-year-old widow with responsibility for four young children. To ease her burden, the Washingtons took the two youngest , Eleanor Parke Custis (b. 1779) and George Washington Parke Custis (b.1781), into their home, and so a second generation of children, a girl and a boy, was raised at Mount Vernon.

Nelly Custis, as Eleanor was called, was nearly five years old at the time of the informal adoption, but she had already spent much of her life at Mount Vernon during the stressful war years. A bright and charming girl, she delighted in and absorbed all the advantages of education and society the Washingtons provided. From most accounts her doting grandmother now guided with a firmer hand, and Nelly grew up with a sophistication and confidence the earlier generation would never have known.

Nelly's little brother, George Washington Parke Custis, was called Wash, Tub, or Boy as a child. As the youngest and only grandson, his health and well being were always under careful scrutiny. He seems to have inherited much of his father's easygoing manner and was something of a trial to his "Grandpappa" Washington, who once described the boy as being "as full of spirits as an eggshell is of meat."[46] Like Jacky before him, Wash knew how to keep his grandmother on his side.

The two older Custis granddaughters, Elizabeth Parke Custis (b. 1775) and Martha Parke Custis (b. 1777), remained in the custody of their mother, who married Dr. David Stuart of Alexandria in 1783. They were frequent visitors to Mount Vernon, sharing in the Washingtons' generosity and affection. Another member of the household was Frances Bassett, called Fanny, the daughter of Mrs. Washington's "greatest favourite" sister, Anna Maria Dandridge Bassett, who had died in 1777. For Mrs. Washington, the presence of her beautiful seventeen-year-old niece at Mount Vernon undoubtedly filled the void that had been left when her daughter Patsy died at the same age ten years earlier. In 1785, Fanny married George Augustine Washington, a nephew of the General's who was working as a secretary and aide to his uncle. The young couple remained in residence, eventually adding three children of their own to the extended family.

Life at Mount Vernon in the mid-1780s was busy, happy and relatively tranquil for the Washingtons. George Washington was overseeing the finishing touches on his much-expanded mansion house and formal gardens and grounds, while Mrs. Washington restored order and regularity to the management of the household. Once again there was a nearly constant stream of relatives and extra guests in the house. The family dining room routinely accommodated any number of visiting nephews and nieces, old acquaintances, well-wishers, and those whom Washington suspected of having come "out of curiosity." In a 1786 letter intended to dissuade his elderly mother from coming to stay, Washington described his home as being like "a well-resorted tavern, as scarcely any strangers who are going from north to south, or from south to north do not spend a day or two at it."[47] A decade later the situation had not changed, as he noted to his secretary, "Unless someone pops in unexpectedly, Mrs. Washington and I will do what has not been [done] by us in nearly 20 years – that is set down to dinner by ourselves."[48]

But Mrs. Washington's domestic contentment was not to last. Although she professed to be unconcerned with "polliticks," her husband continued to maintain a keen interest in public affairs as the new nation tested its foundation. Even so, it was still with some reluctance that Washington consented to preside over the Constitutional Convention that opened in May of 1787. He made the trip to Philadelphia alone, explaining to Robert Morris that "Mrs. Washington has become too Domestick and too attentive to two little Grand Children to leave home."[49] As the structure of the new federal government was hammered out in the debates, it became obvious that Washington was the only choice for its highest office. When formal notification of his election to the presidency arrived at Mount Vernon in April of 1789, Washington dutifully answered the call of his country. He left almost immediately for New York City, then the temporary capital, where on April 30 he was inaugurated first President of the United States of America.

"I am truly sorry to tell that the General is gone to New York," Mrs. Washington had written to her nephew John Dandridge ten days earlier. "Mr. Charles Thompson [Secretary

41

of Congress] came express to him, on the 14th – when, or wheather he will ever come home again god only knows. – I think it was much too late for him to go in to publick life again, but it was not to be avoided. Our family will be deranged, as I must soon follow him."[50] A few weeks after the inauguration, Mrs. Washington, Nelly and Wash set out from Mount Vernon for New York. Robert Lewis, one of Washington's nephews, accompanied the family on their journey and left a poignant account of Mrs. Washington's reluctant departure from home. His diary describes great confusion, excitement and tears at Mount Vernon as a huge number of trunks and boxes were packed for the move. "After an early dinner and making all the necessary arrangements...it brought us to 3 o'clock in the afternoon when we left Mount Vernon," he wrote of their departure on May 16. "The servants of the house and a number of the field Negroes made their appearance to take leave of their mistress. Numbers of these wretches were most affected and my aunt equally so."[51]

Mrs. Washington was greeted with great fanfare at every stop as her party made its way northward. At Baltimore there was a fireworks display and a band that serenaded them until two o'clock in the morning. In Philadelphia, there were celebrations and ceremonies as well as reunions with many old friends from the war years. The President joined the entourage at Elizabethtown Point, New Jersey, to escort them on what can only be described as a triumphal entry by barge into New York City.

It was clear that their countrymen already considered the wife of the President to be a national figure in her own right, and there was an interesting debate over how she should be addressed (the term "First Lady" would not gain currency for another century). While the pro-Federalist *Gazette of the United States* suggested "Marquise" or "Lady," Mrs. Washington remained "Mrs. Washington," setting the precedent for every president's wife thereafter.[52]

Among other precedents established by the Washingtons were their official weekly receptions. The President held a "levee" every Tuesday afternoon, a very formal gathering to which only men were invited. To complement this, Mrs. Washington hosted a Friday evening reception called a "drawing room," a kind of open house that included both politicians and men and women of prominent social standing. The first of these drawing rooms was held just two days after her arrival in New York and was described as being "thick" with people. The protocol of these occasions was carefully worked out to offer gracious hospitality that did not appear ostentatious. The President made a point of always being

Lady Washington's Reception, *by Alexander Hay Ritchie, after Daniel Huntington, 1867.*

present and would appear without his hat or sword as an indication of the informal nature of the affair. Mrs. Washington remained seated as she received her guests, while her husband freely mingled with the company. It was said that he spent most of his time talking with the ladies, claiming it was his only opportunity for this particular pleasure amidst his busy schedule. Refreshments included tea, coffee and cakes and, on at least one occasion, ice cream and lemonade. To close the party, it was reported, Mrs. Washington would stand and announce, "The General always retires at nine, and I usually precede him."[53]

Despite their careful planning to make the entertainments both dignified and democratic, the Washingtons were denounced in the anti-Federalist press for creating the trappings of an American court. Already a reluctant public figure, Mrs. Washington was deeply hurt by these attacks, but she carried on with dignity. Rather than entering into any political debate, she scrupulously honored all of her state obligations with quiet grace and won scores of admirers.

In her private letters to family back home, Mrs. Washington revealed some of her true feelings. Five months after her arrival in New York, she wrote to her niece, Fanny Bassett Washington, "I live a very dull life hear and know nothing that passes in the town – I never goe to the publick place – indeed I think I am more like a state prisoner than anything else, there is certain bounds set for me which I must not depart from – and as I can not doe as I like I am obstinate and stay at home a great deal."[54]

The accounts of her contemporaries present quite a different picture. Abigail Adams, the Vice President's wife, had written to her sister only a short time before, "I took the earliest opportunity…to go and pay my respects to Mrs. Washington…she received me with great ease and politeness. She is plain in her dress, but that plainness is the best of every article. Her Hair is white, her Teeth beautiful, her person rather short than otherways… Her manners are modest and unassuming, dignified and femenine, not a Tincture of ha'ture about her."[55]

In 1790, the seat of government was moved from New York to Philadelphia, and Mrs. Washington had to oversee the move and readjustment of her family to a new city. She also quickly reestablished herself in Philadelphia society, whose members remembered her earlier visits during the dark days of the Revolution when, to quote a writer in the *Pennsylvania Packet,* "she contributed to relieve the cares of our beloved chief and to soothe the anxious moments of his military concern." But despite the attention of strangers and kindnesses of old friends, Mrs. Washington confided in a letter to Mercy Warren, she had grown too old for the "inoscent gayeties of life" in New York and Philadelphia and "had long since placed all prospects of my future worldly happyness in the still enjoyments of the fireside at Mount Vernon."[56]

Her family remained her first priority, and she saw to it that her grandchildren took advantage of the educational and cultural offerings in each of the capital cities. "My grand-children have … good opportunities for acquiring a useful and accomplished education," she told Mrs. Warren. "In their happiness, my own is, in a great measure, involved."[57] In addition to being enrolled in a fashionable girls' school, Nelly had art, dancing and music lessons. The Washingtons had hauled Patsy's old spinet to New York and traded it in for a new, more fashionable pianoforte. In 1793, they ordered a fine harpsichord from London. Years later her brother Wash remembered that Nelly was required to practice her music for long hours: "The poor girl would play and cry, and cry and play…under the immediate eye of her grandmother, a rigid disciplinarian in all things."[58]

George Washington Parke Custis's recollections may have been colored by the passage of time. During their years in Philadelphia, the Custis children's tutor, Tobias Lear, expressed real concern about their attitudes and lack of discipline. "Nelly and Washington have every advantage in point of instructors that this country can give them, and they certainly make good

A period engraving of The Washington Family *by Edward Savage, 1798. General and Mrs. Washington are depicted with Mrs. Washington's two grandchildren, Eleanor and George Washington Parke Custis. In the background is an unidentified slave.*

progress in those things which are taught them," Lear confided to a family friend. "But I apprehend the worst consequences particularly to the boy, from the unbounded indulgence of his grandmamma. The ideas which are insinuated to him at home…that he is born to such noble properties both in estate and otherwise…he is on the road to ruin."[59] The President apparently felt he could not intervene. Addressing Lear's complaints about Wash, he wrote, "Mrs. Washington's happiness is bound up in the boy. Any rigidity used towards him would perhaps be productive of Grievous effects on her."[60] In the fall of 1796, fifteen-year-old Wash went off to Princeton College in New Jersey, but he lasted only a year before he dropped out. Wearily, Washington wrote to Princeton's president to confirm that young Custis would not be returning to school: "He will have only himself to upbraid for any consequences which may follow."[61]

When the Washingtons left home in 1789, they left Mount Vernon in the care of their niece and nephew, Fanny and George Augustine Washington. George Augustine, however, suffered from tuberculosis, a condition that grew progressively worse during the first term of the presidency. Although he had the full support of his uncle, he found he increasingly was unable to keep up with the demands of the estate and finally had to give up his position as Mount Vernon manager altogether. In January 1793, the young Washingtons moved to Eltham, Fanny's family home in New Kent County, where George Augustine died the following month. Fanny and her children returned to northern Virginia and took up residence in a townhouse in Alexandria that Washington provided for them. Although Washington had hired a new manager, William Pearce, to run the operations at Mount Vernon, Mrs. Washington continued to look to Fanny for assistance with domestic details on the estate. Of the hundreds of letters exchanged between them, approximately forty written by Mrs. Washington to Fanny survive, each one spilling over with family news, advice, household directions, and expressions of affection and concern. The Washingtons were overjoyed when Fanny married Washington's longtime secretary, Tobias Lear, in the late summer of 1795. But their happiness was of short duration. Fanny died within a year, possibly of the same affliction her first husband had suffered.

*P*resident Washington had only reluctantly accepted a second term in office. His refusal to run for a third term in 1796 established a precedent that would not be broken for almost a century and a half. "I close my public life on the 4th of March," he wrote to his nephew Robert Lewis in early 1797, "after which no consideration under heaven that I can foresee shall again draw me from the walks of private life." Henrietta Liston, the wife of the British minister to the United States, watched the transition with interest: "In my last I mentioned that Mr. Adams had carried his Ellection for President.... Washington is preparing for retirement with a very cheerful Countenance – Mrs. Washington's heart seems a little melted, as she never expects to see Philadelphia again...."[62]

$\mathcal{G}$eorge and Martha Washington, private citizens again, arrived home at Mount Vernon on March 15, 1797, and began the now familiar process of restoring order and regularity to their home and farm.

"Our circle of friends of course is contracted without any disposition on our part to enter into new friendships, though we have an abundance of acquaintances and a variety of visitors, " Mrs. Washington wrote in a letter to her husband's former secretary David Humphreys soon after their return home.[63] While she continued to be same amiable and attentive hostess she had always been, her travels and experiences had given her a worldliness that impressed a number of her callers. "She loves to talk and talks very well about time past," wrote a Polish traveler, Julian Ursyn Niemcewicz, after a visit in 1798.[64] Noted another visitor, "The extensive knowledge she

This painting titled, Washington and His Family, *features General and Mrs. Washington with two of her grandchildren, Nelly and Eliza, and an unidentified slave. It is by Thomas Prichard Rossiter.*

has gained in this general intercourse with persons from all parts of the world has made her a very interesting companion, and having a vastly retentive memory, she presents an entire history of half a century."[65]

Joshua Brookes, a young English visitor in February 1799, was also captivated by the mistress of Mount Vernon: "[The General] introduced Mrs. Washington [who was] dressed in a Mazareen blue satin gown with three belts over her handkerchief across the body, about five feet high, rather lusty than spare, of respectable appearance, cheerful, about 70 years of age, mildness and affability depicted in her countenance. [She] enquired for news, said she was no politician but liked to read the newspapers, wore a loose cap, hair combed straight, grey locks, sat about half an hour when she went out....Of the whole [family], Mrs. Washington and Miss Custis pleased me most, especially the former. Her affability, free manner and mild, placid countenance brought vividly to my mind my dear mother and I thought I saw in both resignation to God with the pure spirit of religion, humility, meekness, etc...."[66]

There is evidence in surviving manuscripts that some of the letters Mrs. Washington wrote to her more socially prominent correspondents, such as Mercy Warren and Elizabeth Powel, were drafted for her by her husband and then carefully copied out in her less elegant hand before they were sent. One revealing example is the letter she wrote in 1798 to Sally Cary Fairfax, a neighbor from the colonial days (and probably the object of Washington's infatuation before his marriage) who had long ago moved to England. The letter that was sent faithfully follows the elegant diction of Washington's draft: "I was a kind of perambulator during eight or nine years which I resided at the seat of the general government, occupied in scenes more busied, tho no more happy than in the tranquil employment of rural life, with which my days will close." But in a last paragraph Mrs. Washington diverted somewhat from what her husband had written and added her own words to elaborate on the subjects closest to her heart: "With respect to my own family, it will not, I presume, be new to you to hear that my son died in the Fall of 1781. – He left four fine children; three Daughters and a son, a fine promising youth now. –The two eldest of the girls are marred and have children, the second, Patty [Martha], marred before her elder sister; she has two fine children boath girls. – the eldest, Elizabeth marred Mr Law a man of fortune from the East Indies and Brother to the Bishop of Carlyle – she has a daughter. Martha marred Mr Thomas Peter son of Robert Peter of Georgetown, who is also very wealthy. – boath live in the Federal City. – the youngest daughter Eleanor is yet single, and lives with me, having done so from an infant, as has my grandson George Washington – now turned of seventeen – except when at college; to three of which he has been...."[67] The following winter, on February 22, 1799, Eleanor Parke Custis married Lawrence Lewis, the son of George Washington's sister, in a candlelight ceremony at Mount Vernon. They had chosen the date to coincide with George Washington's sixty-seventh birthday, which would prove to be his last.

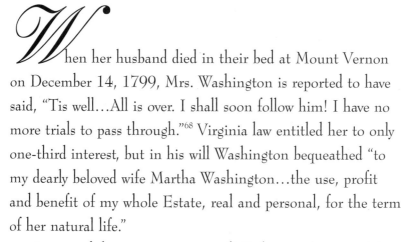

When her husband died in their bed at Mount Vernon on December 14, 1799, Mrs. Washington is reported to have said, "Tis well...All is over. I shall soon follow him! I have no more trials to pass through."[68] Virginia law entitled her to only one-third interest, but in his will Washington bequeathed "to my dearly beloved wife Martha Washington...the use, profit and benefit of my whole Estate, real and personal, for the term of her natural life."

As one of the seven executors of Washington's estate, Mrs. Washington shouldered the special burden of Washington's second provision, which was the granting of freedom to all of the slaves he held "in his own right." In consideration of their intermarriages with the "dower" slaves (those bound to Mrs. Washington and the Custis heirs) Washington decreed that the manumission was to take place upon the death of his wife. Perhaps unwittingly, he had left Mrs. Washington in an untenable position and she moved ahead to arrange for the legal emancipation of the Washington slaves, which took effect on January 1, 1801.

Following an old custom, Mrs. Washington closed off the second-floor bedroom she had shared with her husband in the south wing of the house and moved into a small chamber on the third floor. Her grandchildren, Wash and Nelly, remained in residence, along with Nelly's husband, Lawrence Lewis, and their infant daughter, Frances Parke. It is believed that it was after her husband's death that Mrs. Washington destroyed the bulk of the voluminous correspondence exchanged between them during nearly forty-one years of marriage, thus securing finally and forever a measure of the privacy she had always desired.

Although Mrs. Washington would have preferred obscurity in her last years, Mount Vernon had already become a mecca for Americans and visitors from abroad who now came to pay homage at Washington's tomb. With the help of her grandchildren, she continued to receive visitors with the gracious hospitality that characterized her earlier years. Her loss had left its mark, however. Her old friend, Henrietta Liston, visited Mount Vernon in the summer of 1800, reporting afterwards that Mrs. Washington had "received us with her usual kindness, and not without tears…our spirits were much dampened, and I listened with tender interest to a sorrow, which she said was truly breaking her heart."[69] Mrs. William Thornton, after a visit, also expressed concern over Mrs. Washington's broken spirit, but noted that "the same order & regularity is observed as when the Genl was living."[70]

One of the most telling portraits of Mrs. Washington in her last years was written by the Reverend Manasseh Cutler of Massachusetts, who called on her in January 1802: "Mrs. Washington appears much older than when I saw her last at Philadelphia, but her countenance is very little wrinkled and remarkably fair for a person of her years. She conversed with great ease and familiarity, and appeared as much rejoiced at receiving our visit as if we had been her nearest connections…. We were all Federalists, which evidently gave her particular pleasure. Her remarks were pointed, and sometimes very sarcastic, on the new order of things and the present administration [of Thomas Jefferson].... She spoke frequently of the General with great affection, viewing herself as left alone, her life protracted, until she had become a stranger in the world. She repeatedly remarked the distinguished mercies heaven still bestowed upon her, for which she had daily cause of gratitude, but she longed for the time to follow her departed friend."[71]

By the spring of 1802, visitors were reporting an alarming decline in Mrs. Washington's health. When Thomas Cope, a visitor from Philadelphia, arrived at Mount Vernon on May 20, he learned from her doctor who had been in residence for a fortnight that Mrs. Washington was suffering from a severe fever and not expected to survive. With most of her immediate family gathered at her bedside, death finally came on May 22, 1802. Among the mourners was Thomas Law, husband of her granddaughter Eliza Parke Custis, who described the sad scene in a letter to his son: "Fortitude & resignation were display'd throughout, she met death as a relief from the infirmities & melancholy of old age...."[72] Following private funeral services at Mount Vernon on May 25, Martha Washington was buried beside her husband in the old family vault. A line from her obituary that appeared in the Alexandria paper on that day underscored the essential role she had played in her life: "She was the worthy partner of the worthiest of men."[73]

ENDNOTES

1   MW to Mercy Otis Warren, December 26, 1789. *"Worthy Partner":
    The Papers of Martha Washington*, comp. Joseph E. Fields (Westport,
    CT: Greenwood Press, 1994) [hereafter *Worthy Partner*], 224.

2   *New Letters of Abigail Adams, 1788-1801*, ed. Stewart Mitchell
    (Boston: Houghton Mifflin Co., 1947), 15.

3   Manuscript journal of Eleanor Agnes Lee, entry for March 23, 1856,
    Virginia Historical Society. Cited in Mary P. Couling, *The Lee Girls*
    (Winston-Salem, NC: John F. Blair, Publishers, 1987), 57.

4   Wilson Miles Cary, "The Dandridges of Virginia," *William and Mary
    Quarterly* [first series], vol. 5, no. 1 (July 1896):30.

5   Mechal Sobel, *The World They Made Together: Black and White Values
    in Eighteenth-Century Virginia* (Princeton, NJ: Princeton University
    Press, 1987), 150-152.

6   Custis Papers, Virginia Historical Society. Cited in Douglas Southall
    Freeman, *George Washington: A Biography*, 7 vols. (New York: Charles
    Scribner's Sons, 1948-1951), 2:297.

7   John Power to Daniel Parke Custis, n.d. [probably 1749], in George
    Washington Parke Custis, *Recollections and Private Memoirs of
    Washington* (New York: Derby & Jackson, 1860), 20n.

8   Daniel Parke Custis to John Mercer, no date given; transcribed by
    Mercer in a letter to Martha Custis, January 4, 1758. *Worthy Partner*,
    31. For a discussion of the Dunbar-Parke-Custis case, see Freeman,
    2:279-292.

9   MW to Robert Cary & Co. and MW to John Hanbury & Co., August
    20, 1757. *Worthy Partner*, 5-6.

10 John Tayloe to William Byrd III, April 4, 1758. *The Correspondence of
    the Three William Byrds of Westover, Virginia, 1684-1776*, ed. Marion
    Tinling (Charlottesville: The University Press of Virginia, 1977),
    2:646, 646n.

11 GW to Richard Washington, April 5, 1758. *Papers of George
    Washington*, Colonial series, 5:112.

12 MW to Robert Cary & Company, [1758]. *Worthy Partner*, 25-26.

13 Address from the Officers of the Virginia Regiment, December 31,
    1758. *Papers of George Washington*, Colonial series, 6:178-180.

14 Custis, *Recollections*, 502.

15 Robert Stewart to GW, January 16, 1759. *Papers of George Washington,* Colonial series, 6:187-188.

16 GW to Richard Washington, September 20, 1759. *Papers of George Washington,* Colonial series, 6:359.

17 MW to Mrs. Shelbury, August 1764. *Worthy Partner,* 148; MW to Mrs. S. Thorpe, [July 15, 1772]. *Worthy Partner,* 151.

18 GW to Marie Joseph P. Y. R. G. Du Motier Lafayette, June 10, 1786. *Papers of George Washington,* Confederation series, 4:105.

19 Lund Washington to GW, January 17, 1776. *Papers of George Washington,* Revolutionary war series, 3:129.

20 Susan Gray Detweiler, *George Washington's Chinaware,* prologue and epilogue by Christine Meadows (New York: Harry N. Abrams, 1982), 13-14.

21 MW to Anna Maria Dandridge Bassett, August 28, 1762. *Worthy Partner,* 147.

22 GW to Burwell Bassett, June 20, 1773. *Papers of George Washington,* Colonial series, 9:243.

23 GW to the Jonathan Boucher, May 30, 1768. *Papers of George Washington,* Colonial series, 8:89-90.

24 Jonathan Boucher to GW, December 18, 1770. *Papers of George Washington,* Colonial series, 8:414; Jonathan Boucher to GW, January 19, 1773. *Papers of George Washington,* Colonial series, 9:161.

25 GW to Benedict Calvert, April 3, 1773. *Papers of George Washington,* Colonial series, 9:209.

26 GW to Myles Cooper, December 15, 1773. *Papers of George Washington,* Colonial series, 9:406-407.

27 Edmund Pendleton to _____, [September 1774?], in *The Letters and Papers of Edmund Pendleton, 1734-1803,* coll. and ed. David John Mays (Charlottesville: The University Press of Virginia, 1967), 1:98

28 Family tradition states that following GW's death and before her own, MW burned the vast majority of correspondence that had been exchanged between them. The texts of the three letters of GW to MW that survive are published in *Worthy Partner:* June 18, 1775 (pp.159-160); June 23, 1775 (p. 161); and October 1, 1782 (p. 188). The October 1782 letter is a short note of introduction for a James Brown of Providence, Rhode Island, written from Verplanks Point. According to a note on the verso of the letter, it remained in the possession of the bearer and was never delivered to MW at Mount Vernon. Only two

short notes written by MW to GW are known to have survived. One, a signed note added to the bottom of a letter written by Lund Washington to GW, March 30, 1767, is published in *Worthy Partner,* 149. The other is an unsigned note in MW's hand written on the back of a letter from John Parke Custis to GW, September 11, 1777. See *Papers of George Washington,* Revolutionary war series, 11:203n.

29 GW to MW, June 18, 1775. *Papers of George Washington,* Revolutionary war series, 1:3-5. Original in the collection of the Tudor Place Foundation.

30 GW to John Augustine Washington, June 20, 1775. *Papers of George Washington,* Revolutionary war series, 1:19-20.

31 GW to MW, June 23, 1775. *Papers of George Washington,* Revolutionary war series, 1:27. Original in the collection of the Mount Vernon Ladies' Association.

32 MW to Elizabeth Ramsay, December 30, 1775. *Worthy Partner,* 164.

33 Mercy Otis Warren to Abigail Adams, April 17, 1776. *Adams Family Correspondence,* ed. L.H. Butterfield (Cambridge: The Belknap Press of Harvard University Press, 1963), 1:385.

34 MW to Anna Maria Bassett, January 31, 1776. *Worthy Partner,* 167.

35 GW to John A. Washington, May 31, 1776. *Papers of George Washington,* Revolutionary war series, 4:413.

36 John Parke Custis to MW, August 21, 1776. *Worthy Partner,* 170.

37 Nathanael Greene to Catharine Greene, April 8, 1777. *The Papers of General Nathanael Greene,* ed. Richard K. Showman (Chapel Hill: The University of North Carolina Press, 1980), 2:54.

38 Martha Dangerfield Bland to Frances Bland Randolph, April 12, 1777 [sentence structure and punctuation regularized]. In *Proceedings of the New Jersey Historical Society*, July 1933:152.

39 Custis, *Recollections*, 403.

40 Lafayette to Adrienne de Noailles de Lafayette, January 6 [1778]. *Lafayette in the Age of the American Revolution: Selected Letters and Papers, 1776-1790,* ed. Stanley D. Idzerda (Ithaca: Cornell University Press, 1977), 1:225.

41 James Thacher, *Military Journal of the American Revolutionary War from 1775 to 1783* (Boston: Richardson and Lord, 1823), 192.

42 MW to Eleanor and John Parke Custis, March 19, [1779] (written 1778). *Worthy Partner,* 181.

43 GW to Colonel Jonathan Trumbull, Jr., November 6, 1781. *Writings of George Washington*, ed. John C. Fitzpatrick, 37:554.

44 MW to Hannah Stockton Boudinot, January 15, 1784. *Worthy Partner*, 193.

45 Ibid.

46 Quoted in Miriam Anne Bourne, *First Family: George Washington and His Intimate Relations* (New York: Norton, 1982), 102.

47 GW to Mary Ball Washington, February 15, 1787. *Papers of George Washington*, Confederation series, 5:35.

48 GW to Tobias Lear, July 31, 1797. *Papers of George Washington*, Retirement series, 1:281.

49 GW to Robert Morris, May 5, 1787. *Papers of George Washington*, Confederation series, 5:171.

50 MW to John Dandridge, April 20, 1789. *Worthy Partner*, 213.

51 Journal of Robert Lewis, May 13-29, 1789. Collection of the Mount Vernon Ladies' Association.

52 *Gazette of the United States*, May 30, 1789. Cited in Betty Boyd Caroli, *First Ladies* (New York: Oxford University Press, 1987), 4, 281.

53 Anne Hollingsworth Wharton, *Martha Washington* (New York: C. Scribner's Sons, 1897), 197; also Stephen Decatur, *Private Affairs of George Washington: From the Records and Accounts of Tobias Lear, Esquire, His Secretary* (New York: Da Capo Press, 1969 [c1933]), 44.

54 MW to Fanny Bassett Washington, October 23, 1789. *Worthy Partner*, 230.

55 *New Letters of Abigail Adams*, 13.

56 MW to Mercy Otis Warren, December 26, 1789. *Worthy Partner*, 223.

57 MW to Mercy Otis Warren, June 12, 1790. *Worthy Partner*, 226.

58 Custis, *Recollections*, 408.

59 Bourne, *First Family*, 135.

60 Ibid., 11, 137.

61 GW to Reverend Samuel Stanhope Smith, October 9, 1797. *Papers of George Washington*, Retirement series, 1:396.

62 Henrietta Liston to her uncle, February [24?], 1797. In Bradford

Perkins, ed. "A Diplomat's Wife in Philadelphia: Letters of Henrietta Liston, 1796-1800," *William and Mary Quarterly*, (Oct. 1956). 608.

63 MW to David Humphreys, June 26, 1797. *Worthy Partner*, 304.

64 Julian Ursyn Niemcewicz, *Under Their Vine and Fig Tree: Travels through America in 1797-1799, 1805*, trans. and ed. Metchie J. E. Budka (Elizabeth, NJ: The Grassman Publishing Company, Inc., 1965), 103.

65 Quoted in Bourne, *First Family*, 195.

66 R.W.G. Vail, ed., "A Dinner at Mount Vernon: From the Unpublished Journal of Joshua Brookes (1773-1859)," *The New-York Historical Society Quarterly* (April 1947):74-75.

67 MW to Sally Cary Fairfax, May 17, 1798. *Worthy Partner*, 315. GW's draft of the letter is in the Washington Papers collection at the Library of Congress.

68 Tobias Lear, *Letters and Recollections of George Washington* (New York: Doubleday, Page & Company, 1906), 135.

69 Irene J. Murray, "Mrs. Liston Returns to Virginia," *Virginia Cavalcade* (Summer 1965):46.

70 "Diary of Mrs. William Thornton" [August 2, 1800]. *Records of the Columbia Historical Society, Washington, D. C.* 10 (1907):174.

71 Manasseh Cutler to his daughter, [1802]. In William Parker Cutler and Julia Perkins Cutler, *Life, Journals and Correspondence of Rev. Manasseh Cutler, LL.D.* (Cincinnati: Robert Clarke & Co., 1888), 2:56-58.

72 Thomas Law to John Law, April 23, 1802. Collection of the Mount Vernon Ladies' Association.

73 *The Alexandria Advertiser and Commercial Intelligencer*, April 25, 1802.

SELECTED BIBLIOGRAPHY

Adams, Abigail. *New Letters of Abigail Adams, 1788-1801*. Edited by
   Stewart Mitchell. Boston: Houghton Mifflin Co., 1947.

Anthony, Carl Sferrazza. *First Ladies: the Saga of the Presidents' Wives and
   Their Power, 1789-1961*. New York: William Morrow and Co., 1990.

Bourne, Miriam Anne. *First Family: George Washington and His Intimate
   Relations*. New York: Norton, 1982.

Brady, Patricia. *George Washington's Beautiful Nelly: The Letters of Eleanor
   Parke Custis Lewis to Elizabeth Bordley Gibson, 1794-1851*. Columbia:
   University of South Carolina Press, 1991.

Britt, Judith S. *Nothing More Agreeable: Music in George Washington's
   Family*. Mount Vernon, VA: The Mount Vernon Ladies' Association of
   the Union, 1984.

Caroli, Betty Boyd. *First Ladies*. New York: Oxford University Press,
   1987.

Couling, Mary P. *The Lee Girls*. Winston-Salem, NC: John F. Blair,
   Publishers, 1987.

Custis, George Washington Parke. *Recollections and Private Memoirs of
   Washington*. New York: Derby & Jackson, 1860.

Decatur, Stephen. *Private Affairs of George Washington: From the Records
   and Accounts of Tobias Lear, Esquire, His Secretary*. New York: Da
   Capo Press, 1969 [c1933].

Detweiler, Susan Gray. *George Washington's Chinaware*. Prologue and
   epilogue by Christine Meadows. New York: Harry N. Abrams, 1982.

Flexner, James Thomas. *George Washington*. 4 vols. Boston: Little, Brown,
   1965-1972.

Freeman, Douglas Southall. *George Washington: A Biography*. 7 vols. New
   York: 1948-1951.

Harris, Malcolm Hart. *Old New Kent County: Some Account of the Planters, Plantations and Places in New Kent County*. 2 vols. West Point, VA: The author, 1977.

Lear, Tobias. *Letters and Recollections of George Washington*. New York: Doubleday, Page & Company, 1906.

Niemcewicz, Julian Ursyn. *Under Their Vine and Fig Tree: Travels through America in 1797-1799*, 1805. Translated and edited by Metchie J. E. Budka. Elizabeth, NJ: The Grassman Publishing Company, Inc., 1965.

Thane, Elswyth. *Mount Vernon Family*. New York: Crowell-Collier Press, 1968.

Thompson, Mary V. "'An Agreeable Consort for Life': The Wedding of George and Martha Washington." *Historic Alexandria Quarterly*, Fall 2001.

Washington, George. *The Diaries of George Washington*. Edited by Donald Dean Jackson and Dorothy Twohig. 6 vols. Charlottesville: University Press of Virginia, 1976-1979.

Washington, George. *The Papers of George Washington*. Edited by W.W. Abbot, Dorothy Twohig and Philander Chase. (Colonial, Revolutionary War, Confederation, Presidential and Retirement series.) Charlottesville: University Press of Virginia, 1983-.

Washington, George. *The Writings of George Washington*. Edited by John C. Fitzpatrick. 39 vols. Washington, DC: U.S. Government Printing Office, 1931-44.

Washington, Martha. *"Worthy Partner": The Papers of Martha Washington*. Compiled by Joseph E. Fields. Introduction by Ellen McCallister Clark. Westport, CT: Greenwood Press, 1994.

Wharton, Anne Hollingsworth. *Martha Washington*. New York: C. Scribner's Sons, 1897.